MW00628118

MA-ZEL TOV

YOU'RE MARRIED, NOW WHAT?

ESTHER GROSS

FELDHEIM PUBLISHERS

ISBN 978-1-59826-046-5
Copyright © 2013 by Esther Gross
First published in 2013

FELDHEIM PUBLISHERS
208 Airport Executive Park
Nanuet, NY 10954

BOOK DESIGN
Esther Gross

בס״ד

11 Av, 5773

Dear Mrs. Gross, עמו״ש

I was excited to read yet another book in your series entitled "MA-Zel Tov" on the topic of marriage. All the subjects you have addressed in the past are extremely vital, but this topic surpasses them all. Today more than ever – young people especially – need guidance and constant *chizuk* to build relationships that are healthy and that can endure a lifetime.

The well-known *bracha* that we wish every *choson* and *kallah* is to build a *bayis ne'eman b'yisroel*. This aspect of building doesn't end after the first year, or after you've married off your children; it continues every day for a lifetime. Marriage requires a lot of work to construct an edifice lasting throughout future generations.

Our *Chazal* teach us that if a man and woman merit, the Divine Presence of Hashem will reside in their home. Indeed, that's what marriage is all about – creating and building on a daily basis more *kedusha* with the ultimate partner Hashem Himself.

Throughout the *sheva brachos* we refer numerous times to the concept of *simcha*. Rav Shamshon Rafael Hirsch, *zt"l* points out that the word "שמח" (happiness) is closely related to the word "צמח" (growth) reinforcing the idea that joy and growth are inextricably interwoven. As a couple continues to grow and do for each other their joy will increase as well.

My hope is that every day, married couples of all ages will look through your little book and gain spurts of strength to meander through the difficulties we all face. The pictures are refreshing; the *maamarei Chazal*, insightful, and the poems, uplifting. As a couple blends all of these elements together, I am confident that their marriage will be enriched forever more.

The goal isn't to live forever, but rather to create something that will.

With Torah blessings,
Rabbi Dovid Weinberger

In memory of
my revered father
הרה"ח בנימין אליעזר ז"ל
and his Aishes Chayil my mother
מרת צביה יהודית ע"ה
whose selfless devotion to each other
have imbued us, their children
with a closeness which we cherish and treasure greatly.

In honor of
my dear partner in life,
Mordechai, עמו"ש
אהבת תורה and אהבת הבריות whose
make him an extraordinary husband, father and grandfather.
May Hashem grant us *nachas* and the continued ability
to share and grow spiritually, עד מאה ועשרים שנה.

Acknowledgements

I take this opportunity to express my deepest gratitude to Rabbi Dovid Weinberger, שליט"א for taking time out once again from his busy schedule to read my manuscript and for his constant *chizuk* and encouragement.

It is with a deep sense of gratitude and appreciation that I acknowledge the staff at Feldheim Publishers, New York whose guidance and inspiration have motivated me to pursue yet another project. Especially my dearest friend, Suzanne Brandt who so graciously worked on my manuscript from compilation to completion.

I wish to express my sincere gratitude to R' Reuven A. Stone for his support, help and guidance throughout this project.

Special thanks to my wonderful friends Ruthie Vidomlanksi and Rena Laufer for their editorial contributions to this book.

Special thanks to my dearest family and friends. I value and cherish all your support and wisdom. May you be blessed with the best of health and much *yiddishe nachas*.

THE HIGHEST LEVEL OF JOY can only be attained through marriage and one can only become whole through matrimony. When the glass is broken under the *chuppah* all participants proclaim, "Mazel Tov" jubilantly.

A glass is a receiving vessel: one pours into a glass or keeps things in a glass. And so, when the *chuppah* ceremony is completed, the *chasan* (groom) breaks the glass to let everybody know that from now on, he is a giver – one who will do his utmost to give to his wife; she in turn, will reciprocate in the same manner.

We live in a society where we expect instantly "the whole enchilada." You can send a text message to your grocer and get a frozen meal delivered almost instantaneously, pop it into the microwave, serve it on disposable plates and enjoy a scrumptious meal for two. In contrast, a beautiful marriage is a work in progress: by facing each other day by day, working sincerely and courageously together to make things flow.

Of course, there are hurdles along the way, but there should be no room for discouragement. All that is required is genuine effort. We are only obligated to do our part and Hashem will help us with what seems impossible. The Yalkut Shimoni on *Tehillim* 136:13 says, "A person does with his hands and Hashem will bless the works of his hands."

Marriage is the art of making your spouse the most important person in the world. One can only love a person if one gives. "You love the one to whom you give" (Michtav Mi'Eliyahu). Giving requires giving it all you've got: it entails acknowledging your spouse's needs with words, deeds and a pleasant attitude. It is expressions of gratitude, complimenting each other, letting each other win and treating each other with dignity. Giving is keeping your word, listening attentively and acting accordingly to the wishes of your spouse. It is spending special times together, enjoyably and communicating in a loving fashion. It is feeling concern for each other and working together to attain a satisfying relationship.

A healthy relationship involves expressing your feelings in terms of how each can enrich the marriage and by realizing that both of you may not be able to deliver everything, but at least you're showing that you honestly do care to please and appease. Obviously, you'll need some help along the way. We're all novices; every day we encounter new tests. You'll need a wise mentor, Rav and an agenda-free friend who will listen, support and guide you.

Marriage flourishes when both partners honor and appreciate each other's differences. Peace in the home doesn't mean absence of differences, but an attempt to bridge the gap by being open and receptive to each other.

"MA-Zel Tov, You're Married, Now What?" This book is not only for newlyweds but for all married couples. Every age has its own stage of seasons and at each moment we have a chance to reboot, rejuvenate and reaffirm our marriage which is a lifetime commitment.

Certainly we need Hashem's help along the way. Pray to Hashem to help you feel more loving, to be more supportive and considerate; to have the strength to turn negatives into positives; to attain humility so that you can let go of the past and concentrate on the present; to know your own greatness so that you can value your partner's good points; to emulate Hashem Who is compassionate, giving and forgiving.

Marriage is a win-win investment with bountiful prospects. I trust that this little book will serve as your portable therapist and help you prosper in your holy, joint venture.

Esther Gross

MA-ZEL
TOV

ASPIRE
to build a miniature
sanctuary:
Based on commitment
and faithfulness,
On the grounds
of trust and openness,
In the sacred union
of matrimony.

Let no sadness come through this gate.
Let no trouble come to this dwelling.
Let no fear come through this door.
Let no conflict be in this place.
Let this home be filled with the blessing of joy and peace.
(Yismach Moshe)

ברכת הבית

בזה השער לא יבוא צער.
בזאת הדירה לא תבוא צרה.
בזאת הדלת לא תבוא בהלה.
בזאת המחלקה לא תבוא מחלוקת
בזה המקום תהי ברכה ושלום.

קמיע הטחבר ישטח משה

BLOOM

where you're planted.
When you enter your home,
   choose peace and goodwill.
The mezuzah
   on the door is slanted,
As a cue to be
   easygoing and flexible.

ה' יִשְׁמָר צֵאתְךָ וּבוֹאֶךָ מֵעַתָּה וְעַד עוֹלָם (תהילים קכ"א:ח)
Hashem will guard your departure and arrival,
from this time and forever. (Tehillim 121:8)

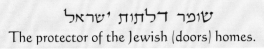

שׁוֹמֵר דַּלְתוֹת יִשְׂרָאֵל
The protector of the Jewish (doors) homes.

COMMUNICATE

your needs effectively.
Speak softly, clearly
and courteously.
If you measure and weigh
your words carefully,
They will be
considered respectfully.

צוֹף דְּבַשׁ אִמְרֵי נֹעַם מָתוֹק לַנֶּפֶשׁ וּמַרְפֵּא לָעָצֶם
(מִשְׁלֵי ט"ז:כ"ד)
Pleasant words are like a honeycomb,
sweet to the soul and health to the bones.
(Misheli 16:24)

DISPLAY
your appreciation
in a tangible way:
A small gift on
a no-occasion day,
Illustrates more than
an artist can portray,
And significantly more than
text messaging can convey.

...וּבְטוֹב הָעוֹלָם נִדוֹן, וְהַכֹּל לְפִי רֹב הַמַּעֲשֶׂה
(פִּרְקֵי אָבוֹת ג:י"ט)

...and the world is judged with goodness,
and everything depends on the abundance of good deeds.

(Pirkei Avos 3:19)

EMULATE

our forefathers'
righteousness:
Fill your home with
noble acts of kindness.
Pray to Hashem
with deep concentration
and yearning.
Allocate a set time
for Torah learning.

על שלשה דברים העולם עומד: על התורה,
ועל העבודה ועל גמילות חסדים (פרקי אבות א:ב)

The world stands on three pillars - on the Torah,
on the service of G-d, and upon acts of lovingkindness. (Pirkei Avos 1:2)

איזו היא עבודה שהיא בלב? הוי אומר זו תפילה (תענית ב:א)

What is the service of the heart? It is prayer. (Taanis 2a)

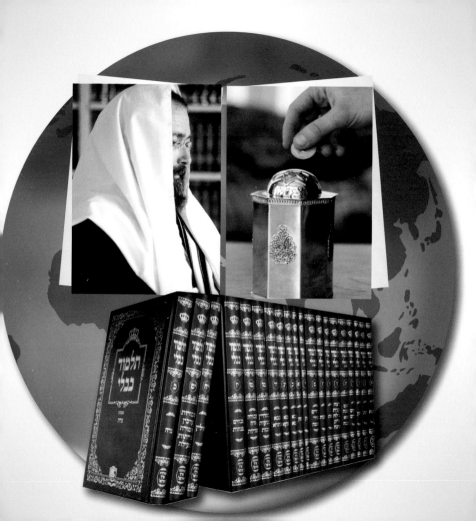

Focus

on being polite and considerate
all the seasons of life,
Unequivocally you'll merit
freedom from strife:
Your marriage will
deepen and thrive,
As you keep your faith
and aspirations alive.

לא מצא הקב"ה כלי מחזיק ברכה לישראל אלא השלום
שנאמר ה' עוז לעמו יתן ה' יברך את עמו בשלום
(עוקצין ג:י"ב)

Great is peace, for which reason the entire Torah was given...
Hashem found no better receptacle for blessing than peace.
(Uktzin 3:12)

GIVING

blesses both, the giver
and the receiver.
Each display
of kindheartedness
Will generate closeness.
What goes around
comes around.

HOPE

will deliver you
through thick and thin.
In good times it gives you
the get-up-and-go to win.
In hard times it showers you
with powers to
transcend difficulties,
While evoking your
dormant capabilities.

קִוִּיתִי ה' קִוְּתָה נַפְשִׁי וְלִדְבָרוֹ הוֹחָלְתִּי (תהילים ק"ל:ה)

I hoped in Hashem, my soul hoped
and I wait for His word. (Tehillim 130:5)

עֶזְרֵנוּ בְּשֵׁם ה' עֹשֵׂה שָׁמַיִם וָאָרֶץ (תהילים קכ"ד:ח)

Our help is through the name of Hashem,
Maker of heaven and earth. (Tehillim 124:8)

INSCRIBE

in your tender hearts
which glow,
Resilience and perseverance
to help each other grow.
Whilst facing turbulence,
Employ your good sense;
Tap into your souls to feel
inner peace and abundance.

אשא כנפי שחר אשכנה באחרית ים:
גם־שם ידך תנחני ותאחזני ימינך
(תהילים קל"ט:ט-י)

Were I to take up wings of dawn, were I to dwell
in the darkest west, there too, Your hand would guide me
and Your right hand would grasp me.
(Tehillim 139:9-10)

Just

as the sand washed
by rain so pure,
Is illuminated at daylight,
So in a marriage when one
is forgiving and mature,
Each day is chock-full
of pleasure and delight.

עולם חסד יבנה (תהילים פ"ט:ג)
The world will be built by acts of lovingkindness. (Tehillim 89:3)

בחכמה יבנה בית ובתבונה יתכונן, ובדעת חדרים ימלאו כל הון יקר ונעים
(משלי כ"ד:ג-ד)
Through wisdom is a house built and by understanding it is established;
and by knowledge are the chambers filled
with all precious and pleasant riches.
(Mishlei 24:3-4)

KNOW

when to speak; your partner
   doesn't always need advice.
Change paths before you
   put your tongue into action.
Genuine empathy is
   listening twice,
And using the gift of speech
   only a fraction.

חכם אינו מדבר לפני מי שהוא גדול ממנו בחכמה,
ואינו נכנס לתוך דברי חברו...

(פרקי אבות ה:ז)

A learned person... does not interrupt the words
of his fellow; he does not answer impetuously;
he asks relevant questions, and replies appropriately ...

(Pirkei Avos 5:7)

LAUGHTER

and joy are healing potions,
They elevate our emotions,
Whereby fine-tuning
   our personalities,
To adjust and adapt to
   life's ever changing melodies.

השמחה תיטיב לגוף כדבר רפואה (פעודת דוד)
A joyous heart heals the body.
(Metzudos Dovid on Mishlei 17:22)

יערב עליו שיחי אנכי אשמח בה
אשירה לה׳ בחיי אזמרה לא-לקי בעודי: (תהילים ק״ד:ל״ג-ל״ד)
I will sing to Hashem while I live,
I will sing praises to my G-d while I endure.
May my words be sweet to Him. I will rejoice in Hashem.
(Tehillim 104:33-34)

MARRIAGE

is like planting a tree:
Persistent nagging
   can sap its energy;
It requires time and space,
To spread and grow
   at its own pace;
Only then can it
   produce fruits plentifully.

כי האדם עץ השדה
(דברים כ:י"ט)

...for man is like a tree of the field.
(Devarim 20:19)

When demands begin, love departs.
(Michtav Me'Eliyahu - Strive for Truth - LovingKindness 6)

OTE:

Treat your partner
    as you would treat yourself.
Even when you're upset,
    get a hold of yourself.
Peace is achievable,
With face-to-face dialogue
    and love that is unconditional.

ואהבת לרעך כמוך (ויקרא י"ט-"ח)

Love your fellow man as your 'self'. (Vayikra 19-18)

The word your 'self' seems redundant.
The Torah is teaching us just as you love yourself (you overlook your own faults)
you should act the same way concerning others. (R' Levi Yitzchok of Berditchov)

❋

זרח בחשך אור (קי"ב:ד) = (752)

Even in darkness a light shines... (Tehillim 112:4)

צפור (a bird) = 376 has the same numerical value as שלום (peace) = 376
Two peaceful birds (2 x 376) chirping in flight
Brighten up the dreary woods at night! = 752 (Author)

OFFER
the mirror
a big bright smile,
It will absolutely
respond in kind.
Kindred spirits discover
after a while,
They evoke reciprocal
good feelings within
each other's heart and mind.

כמים הפנים לפנים כן לב האדם לאדם (משלי כ"ז:י"ט)

As water mirrors the face to the face
so one's heart is reflected back to him by another. (Mishlei 27:19)

דברים היוצאים מן הלב נכנסים אל הלב (מאמר החכם)

Words which emanate from the heart, enter the heart.

(Wisdom from the Sages)

PRIORITIZE,

put first things first.
The first to see the other's
point of view is the noblest.
The first to apologize
is the bravest.
The first to forgive
is the strongest.
The first to move forward
is the happiest.

הלל אומר: הוי מתלמידיו של אהרן אוהב שלום ורודף שלום
אוהב את הבריות ומקרבן לתורה
(פרקי אבות א:י״ב)

Hillel says: be among the students of Aharon,
loving peace and pursuing peace,
loving people and encouraging them to be closer to the Torah.
(Pirkei Avos 1:12)

QUELL

your feelings of wrath.
Everything seems different
    after a good night's sleep.
Gentleness disarms
    the tough and leads to
    a magnificent path,
Where quiet, sun-drenched
    waters run deep.

טוב ארך אפים מגבור ומושל ברוחו מלכד עיר (משלי ט״ז:ל״ב)
He who is slow to anger is better than a mighty man,
and a master of his passions is better than the conquerer of a city.
(Mishlei 16:32)

✳

מענה רך ישיב חמה ודבר עצב יעלה אף (משלי ט״ו:א)
A soft answer turns away wrath, but a distressing word
stirs up anger. (Mishlei 15:1)

RELEASE
your ill feelings
from ages ago,
They are a waste
of time and vitality.
The toil of dropping
a bit of ego,
Beats driving
a truckload of hostility.

כל עבודת השם תלוי בתקון המדות שהם כמו לבוש
למצות וכללי התורה
(אבן שלימה א')

The essence of serving Hashem is self refinement;
they are like garments for the Mitzvos and the Torah.
(Even Sheleimah 1)

SET

a warm environment,
By viewing each glitch
   as a challenging event.
Even if you see things differently,
You can sort out issues skillfully.
Similar to a jumbled Rubik's cube:
   each dice facing a different direction,
However with some smart moves
   it can be restored to
   its original configuration.

בשלשה דברים אדם פשתנה מחבירו, בקול במראה ובדעת
(סנהדרין ל"ח עמוד א)
In three things man differs from his fellow man:
in voice, appearance and mind.
(Sanhedrin 38a)

THINK

things through:
Stop before making
a major irrevocable change.
Don't allow your impulses
to get the better of you.
Keep a log of your concerns
and consult a wise friend
and Torah sage.

עשה לך רב וקנה לך חבר (פרקי אבות א:ו)
Provide yourself with a Torah scholar; acquire yourself a friend...
(Pirkei Avos 1:6)

...מרבה עצה מרבה חכמה (פרקי אבות ב:ח)
The more counsel, the more understanding ...
(Pirkei Avos 2:8)

UNITE

as allies to achieve
a common goal.
Exchange the haughtiness
of "I" and "me"
With the nobleness
of "us" and "we".
Marriage is two complete halves
of one complete whole.

...הנה מה טוב ומה נעים שבת אחים גם יחד
(תהילים קל"ג:א)

...Behold how good and how pleasant
is the dwelling of brothers also in unity.
(Tehillim 133:1)

VERBALIZE

your warm sentiments.
Set aside unruffled times
   to discuss daily events.
Serve up a tea for two,
With freshly baked goods too.
Relish these nurturing moments:
   they're beyond compare,
Someday they will be memories
   you hold so dear.

הלשון קולמוס הלב, ושליח המצפון
(חובות הלבבות: שער הבחינה ה)

The tongue is the heart's pen and the mind's messenger.
(Duties of the Heart, Second Gate: Reflection Chapter 5)

WEED

out unrealistic expectations
and critique
Every waking hour
of the day and week.
Mind and mend
a misunderstanding
With the threads
of peacemaking
and problem solving.

...יהי כבוד חברך חביב עליך כשלך: ואל תהי נוח לכעוס...
(פרקי אבות ב':ט"ו)

Let your fellow's honor be as dear as your own,
and do not anger easily...
(Pirkei Avos 2:15)

XEMPLIFY

refined character traits,
We were each created
with a divine spark.
Highlight the goodness that
your partner radiates,
Always enter or exit
your home with blessings
and a kind remark.

ואמרתם כה לחי ואתה שלום וביתך שלום וכל אשר לך שלום
(שמואל א':כ"ה-כ"ו)
...Acclaim: peace be upon your house
and peace be upon all that is yours! (1 Shmuel 25:26)

✿

...צאו וראו איזו הי'א דרך טובה שידבק בה האדם ...רבי' אלעזר אומר: לב טוב...
(פרקי אבות ב':י"ג)
Go out and distinguish which is the good path to which
a man should cling... Rabbi Elazar said: a good heart... (Pirkei Avos 2:13)

YOUTH

continues when you're
   both older
   but young at heart,
When beginning each morning
   you make a fresh start:
Motivated to preserve
   your deep mutual affection
   and admiration,
As on the day of your
   wedding celebration.

אשת חיל מי ימצא ורחק מפנינים מכרה:
בטח בה לב בעלה ושלל לא יחסר (משלי ל"א:י'-י"א)

A woman of valor who can find? For her price is beyond pearls.
Her husband's heart relies on her
and he shall lack no fortune. (Mishlei 31:10-11)

ZERO
in on a wedding so royal:
It was the marriage between
Hashem and Klal Yisroel.
When we received the Torah
and vowed to make
a personal transformation,
It was a moment in time –
linking generation to generation.
As we bolster our marriages
with our partners buoyantly,
May we prosper materially
and spiritually, exultantly.

...וֶהְיִיתֶם לִי סְגֻלָּה מִכָּל הָעַמִּים כִּי לִי כָּל הָאָרֶץ (שמות י״ט:ה)
... and you shall be My treasure amongst the nations,
for the entire world is Mine. (Shemos 19:5)

LET US MAKE A DEAL

When Moishe got engaged,
   he told his wife-to-be:
"With all sincerity,
   it would mean the world to me,
If you would just fulfill
   my very small request,
I assure you what I say,
   I do not say in jest.

"Let us make a deal,
   before our ceremony,
So our lives will not be filled
   with remorse or acrimony.
At all costs – no matter what –
   I never want to fight.

Promise me, today forth:
   you always will be right."

So, after their wedding day,
   Chavi was treated like a queen;
Side-by-side, together
   a happier couple – never seen.
She was always glad to please,
   leaving no chore undone.
Happily making peace –
   an *Aishes Chayil* bar none.

One night Chavi awoke
   completely distraught and vexed
Wondering why she was
   so befuddled and perplexed.
In the early morn',
   after much deliberation,
She came to
   an astonishing realization:

LET US MAKE A DEAL

She was so uneasy
  about always being right,
And now it was clear
  not everything was black
  and white!
Moishe thought he was dreaming
  when he heard his wife's request:
"A smidgen of honesty
  will keep us at our best.

"I am not always right
  and you are not always wrong.
So let us make a deal
  that will keep our marriage strong:
I never want us to fight
  no matter what transpires;
So you be right half the time,
  if that's what it requires."

And so after many years
  in harmony they live;
Compromising with each other,
  kindnesses they give –

With children who have grown
  to be reverent and kind;
Hashem has blessed them truly:
  health, wealth and peace of mind.

Committed and devoted
  through challenges they've borne;
With sterling reputations
  because of strife foresworn.

———⟨ᴥ⟩———

Together they have built
  a *Bais Ne'eman B'Yisroel,*
A sparkling edifice where
  the *Shechina* surely dwells.

(based on a true story)

MARRIAGE MOTIVATIONAL MUSINGS

Popular & Original Sayings
for Success in Marriage

A good marriage is made up of two good people.

A house is not a home, unless it's shared with others.

A sweet disposition, will with application, surmount any difficulty.

ABSENCE makes the heart grow fonder, but presence makes the heart stronger.

ADDRESS the problem, not the person.

ALWAYS be there for each other. A successful relationship needs both people believing in each other.

ATTITUDE is mind over matter. If you don't mind, it doesn't matter.

AWARENESS makes us appreciate life and the simple pleasures that fill it with splendor.

BE accommodating like a reed rather than stiff like a cedar.

BEFORE a disagreement escalates, ask yourself, "How important is it?"

BELIEVE: it will give you the power to achieve whatever you conceive.

BE a lifter, not a leaner.

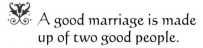

Attentiveness ❦ Benevolence ❦ Commitment

BLESSED are the flexible, for they will not get bent out of shape.

CHARACTER is greater than intellect.

CHOOSE your attitude and your actions to fashion a marvelous life.

DO not go to sleep without a positive remark.

DON'T stretch the truth, it might snap back at you.

ENCOURAGEMENT and forgiveness are gifts you give to yourself.

EVERY story has three sides: mine, yours and the truth.

EVERY minute you're angry you lose sixty seconds.

FAITH is the key that keeps you together in the storm of life.

FOCUS on what's right and not on who's right.

FORGET your own mistakes and don't recall those of your partner.

FOUR hands can do more than two.

FRET today, regret tomorrow.

Dedication ❧ Empathy ❧ Flexibility

- GENEROSITY is the only investment that never fails.

- GIVE unconditionally.

- GIVEN enough time, running water can hollow out a stone.

- HALVING your wants, quadruples your wealth.

- HAPPINESS in marriage comes when both spouses give to each other.

- HAPPINESS flourishes when there is union in diversity.

- HAPPY couples fight; they fight for their marriage.

- HOME brings you warmth like the sun.

- HOME is a safe haven.

- HONESTY and trust are the foundations of a good marriage.

- IF you do not say it, you will not have to unsay it.

- IF you want more of something, then give more of that thing.

- IN marriage, the little things are often the big things.

- INITIATE mending a misunderstanding.

- JOY shared is doubled.

Gentleness ❦ Humor ❦ Insightfulness ❦ Joy

JUST do what is right. Be just in all your actions, remembering that there is always room for mercy.

KINDNESS is the oil that takes the friction out of a marriage.

KINDNESS helps you to understand others and clears feelings of hurt and distrust.

LIFE is not a problem to be solved but a gift to be enjoyed.

LIFE is 10% what happens to you and 90% how you react to it.

LIFE's beautiful moments come unannounced.

LISTENING means hearing and adhering.

LISTENING: the greatest compliment you can give is your undivided attention.

LOVE exits when demands enter.

MARRIAGE is a common search for the good and the beautiful.

MARRIAGE: what to expect when you're accepting.

Kindliness ❧ Loyalty ❧ Maturity ❧ Nobility

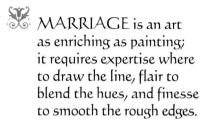 MARRIAGE is an art as enriching as painting; it requires expertise where to draw the line, flair to blend the hues, and finesse to smooth the rough edges.

MARRIAGE is not about marrying the right person, but being the right partner.

MARVEL at each other's talents.

MEMORIES are your most treasured possessions.

MEND your own business.

MENTION something uplifting.

MIGHTY oaks from little acorns grow.

MIRACLES multiply with sharing.

MOST of the things you worry about never happen.

NEVER give up on yourself or others.

ONLY through the vicissitudes of life is marriage strengthened.

OPEN your mind and heart; with wisdom and warmth you can overcome difficulties together.

Optimism ❧ Poise ❧ Quietude

PATIENCE is a virtue, which won't hurt you.

PEACE is always present. You just have to look for it.

PEOPLE who speak with tact have less to retract.

PRACTICE being allies with common goals.

PRAYER and patience are the two key pillars to a solid marriage.

PROMOTE but never demote yourself or others.

QUICKLY forgive and be quick to ask for forgiveness.

REACH down and lift others up.

REMEMBER: Compromise, Compassion and Commitment will help you come to an agreement.

RELEASE your negative attitudes, unhealthy habits, nagging worries, stressful thoughts and feel rejuvenated and restored.

SHARE what's really going on. Your partner is not a mind reader.

SILENCE is the hardest argument to refute.

Reliability ❦ Supportiveness ❦ Tactfulness

- SPEAKING softly can usually command attention.

- SPOTLIGHT your spouse's strengths.

- SIGHT and insight are what you need to have a fruitful life.

- SUCCESSFUL marriages take time for solitude.

- SUPPRESSING a moment of anger can save a day of sorrow.

- TEN words: "My dear, I was wrong. I apologize. Please forgive me".

- THE more you listen, the more your partner will respect and value your opinion.

- TREAT your partner as if they were what they could be.

- TRUST is a two-way street: each partner has to be worthy of trust, just as he must trust his partner.

- UNEXPECTED! Do something special to spice up your marriage.

- VALUE your relationships – they add meaning to your life.

Unity ❧ Vision ❧ Willingness

WEDDING: the first two letters spell WE to accentuate that WE are not meant to fly solo. From this day on it will not be I or ME, but WE.

WHEN "if" and "when" are planted, nothing grows.

WHEN both partners work on their marriage, it becomes twice as good.

WITH every kind deed, you're sowing a seed.

WITHOUT faith nothing is possible; with it everything is possible.

YOU can't expect to win the jackpot if you don't buy a lottery ticket.

YOU don't need an invitation to help others.

YOU climb the highest when you help someone else up.

XPERIENCE is the best teacher.

YOU do not always have to leave home to take a vacation.

ZEAL gives us the courage to move on and experience constant success.

Xuberance ❧ Youthfulness ❧ Zest